Me & My Person

A Dog's Memoir of Love and Loss

Luke Gibson
Illustrated by Lizette Duvenage

Me & My Person

A Dog's Memoir of Love and Loss

Written by Luke Gibson
Illustrated by Lizette Duvenage
Edited by Betsy Thorpe

Scripture quotations are taken from the New International Version (John 3:16) and the King James Version (Psalm 23:4).

Published by Luke Gibson, Charlotte, NC

Soft Cover ISBN: 979-8-9917475-1-6
Hard Cover ISBN: 979-8-9917475-0-9
E-Book ISBN: 979-8-9917475-2-3

Library of Congress Control Number: 2024924012

In loving memory of Gip Gibson

Me & My Person is dedicated to anyone who has lost someone special. May you find strength and healing through love.

Special thanks to Patty Wischan-Rosen for giving me the confidence to share my story.

Special thanks to Virginia Hart for sharing her knowledge and for encouraging me each step of the way.

~ Luke Gibson ~

Dear Reader,

My name is Luke. As you can see, I am a Golden Retriever dog. I am also a very happy dog. I was adopted by a man who loved me without limits. It was extraordinary. I loved him back like only a dog can love—with my whole heart and being.

I want to share this true story with you. It is a story about growing up, about amazing love and loyalty, and also about loss and hope.

It is my life story, so I will start at my beginning...

I was born in Harmony, North Carolina, on a pretty Amish farm. I had four fluffy, furry brothers and two sweet sisters—all of us Golden Retrievers.

My mother and grandmother raised us. As little puppies, we loved to play out on the green grass and wear each other out. Sometimes we got so tired that we just fell asleep right there on the soft grass.

I jumped on my mother and grandmother and nipped at them with my tiny, sharp teeth. Grandmother would snarl at

me when I tried to play with her. She thought I was too sassy. My mother was more patient with me. She nuzzled me and cuddled me.

I never knew my father, but I was told his name was Turbo Diesel. Later, when I grew to be an extra-large, super-strong Golden Retriever dog, I wondered if his name reflected his size and strength and whether I looked like him.

One day, while I was playing on the grass with my brothers and sisters, a lady, her husband, and their old dog came to visit us. They came back to visit a couple more times.

On the last visit, only the husband and the dog came. The man called me to him. I ran over to his side, and before I knew it, he'd picked me up and put me into the back seat of his car with the old dog!

I didn't want to leave my family, and I really wasn't sure about going with this man and his dog. My mom had explained that often puppies didn't stay with their birth moms—instead, they were adopted by humans so that the puppies could grow up and help them. I guessed it was my time to do that. It still wasn't easy. I was so upset that I threw up all

over the dog on the ride to their house.

When we got to my new home, I didn't like the lady very much. The man was so nice to me. I couldn't help but like him.

The man spent hours holding me in his lap and telling me what a smart puppy I was. He taught me how to "sit" and "lie down," and when I did that, I got a little treat! I never did quite get the "come" command, but he loved me anyhow. I also learned that the man's name was Gip, the lady's name was Clement, and the dog's name was Mookie.

I grew to love the man, Gip, with my whole heart.

It took a while for Clement to accept me, and for me to accept her. I was a handful, and I was not too nice to Mookie. I wanted to play with Mookie. I jumped on her and snapped at her, but she was too old and grouchy to play with me. Clement scolded me when I was mean to Mookie, and that frustrated me. Then, one day, I didn't see Mookie anymore—I'm not sure what happened, just that she was gone. This made both Gip and Clement sad.

I was still very young and full of energy and didn't know how to act around others. Gip continued to work with me. Clement took me to a puppy training class to learn to "come," "stay," and "leash walk." I didn't learn anything

because all I wanted to do was play with the other dogs. Behaving was boring.

Gip spent hours and hours with me, patiently trying to help me adjust to this big change. On the farm, I could run freely outside with my dog family. Now I was learning to live in a small house with people who took me for walks on a leash.

I destroyed just about everything in sight: I dug up Gip's beautiful garden, chewed on the furniture, and even tore up credit cards and pictures lying on tables. I also enjoyed stealing something personal of theirs and running away with it. I would give it back only when they offered me a treat in exchange. It was all such fun, but I could tell that my bad behavior upset both Gip and Clement. It caused arguments between them, but I just couldn't help myself. I had lots of energy and needed to play and exercise out my wiggles. I was such a wild puppy. At one point it got so bad that Clement tried to talk Gip into getting rid of me. He refused. He told her he'd chosen me, and he was NOT going to give up on me.

At that moment in my puppy life, when I saw how Gip continued to stick up for me, I chose Gip as "my person." We howled together each morning to greet the day, I followed him from room to room with my tail wagging, and

he invited me to lie down on the sofa with him when we both needed a rest. I just loved being with him.

Clement found a solution to my excess energy problem and my need to play all day: she started taking me to doggy daycare. At first, I was shy and scared and stayed in the corner, but then I made some friends.

I began to like doggy daycare so much that I looked forward to going! In the mornings, when Gip reached for my leashes to get me ready, I'd spin and jump with excitement. (Because I was a big dog and not well-behaved, I needed two leashes. One is called a "gentle leader" harness that goes around my nose, and the other leash snaps onto my collar.)

Clement dropped me off at daycare in the mornings and then came back for me in the afternoons. When she brought me back home, I knew that I'd find food in my bowl, a KONG full of peanut butter, and cookies waiting for me. After eating, I'd stretch out on the soft rug under the dining room table and take a giant nap. I was so worn out.

The love and care from Gip and Clement were awesome. They rarely left me by myself. Sometimes they went to a doctor's appointment or out to lunch, but they were gone for no more than a couple of hours.

Time passed happily until my person, Gip, began to have trouble walking. Soon he had to use a wheelchair. He still let me lie on his lap on the sofa, and he petted me all the time, but I could tell he was hurting.

Then one day, just like any other, Gip fell. Clement wasn't at home, and I didn't know how to help. I ran over to Gip and put my whole body on his, all 120 pounds of me! He struggled to get me off of him, but I didn't want him to get up and fall again. I was hoping Clement would get home soon and help. Instead, Gip managed to get up so that she never saw him on the floor. It hurt me, though, to see him in pain.

I heard Gip tell Clement he was dying. He had something called "cancer." She seemed to listen without really believing that it was true, but I heard, and it made me very sad... very, very sad. I loved him—Gip was my person, and I didn't want anything to happen to him.

Clement took good care of Gip when he was ill. She fixed him delicious meals and made sure he took all his medicine.

She also wanted Gip to have her faith, so she shared what she believed almost daily.

When Clement was in high school, her loving parents and grandmother had each

passed away, all within one year. She had suffered terribly.

One day, Clement had an amazing dream about Jesus which she shared with a minister. He helped her understand that her Christian family was in Heaven, and he explained how much God loved them. This gave her peace.

The minister asked Clement if she believed that Jesus Christ died on the cross for her and that He rose from the dead. He explained that by believing in Jesus Christ, she too would have eternal life and see her family again. That day, Clement accepted Jesus Christ as her personal Lord and Savior.

This is why Clement believed with all of her heart that Gip needed to accept Jesus as his personal Savior before he too passed away.

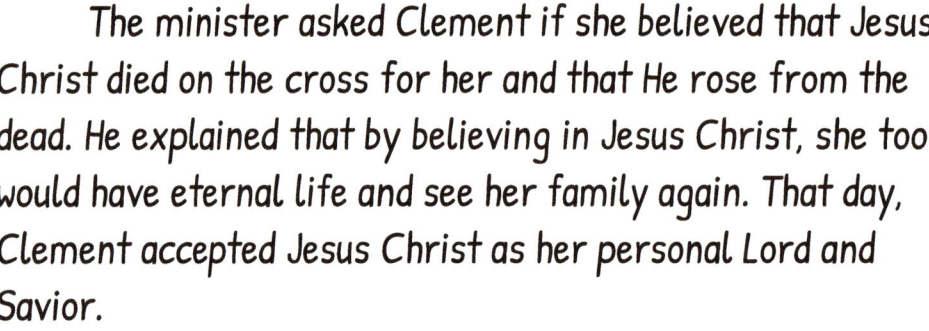

"For God so loved the world
That he gave his one and only Son,
That whoever believes in him
Shall not perish but have eternal life."

—John 3:16

I saw Gip writing notes to Clement while he was ill. He told me he wrote to her about how much he loved her. He wrote that he had accepted Jesus and would see her "there." Gip included two Scripture verses Clement had given him, plus photos of them together during happy times. He said he was leaving these love notes for Clement to find after his passing to reassure her that he would see her again in Heaven. Gip talked to me a lot while we sat side-by-side on the couch. He didn't think I understood what he was telling me, but I did.

When Gip was hurting, he sometimes pushed me aside and yelled at me. I didn't let that make any difference. I knew he did those things because he was in pain. I tried not to bug Gip, but I wanted to show him how much I loved him.

I still needed Gip. He was the one who wouldn't give up on me. He loved me through the bad times. He always defended me, he had my back, and I hope he knew that I always had his. Gip was my person. I loved him so much.

It seemed like the years I'd spent with Gip went by too fast. We still sang our howling songs together, and I still sat on his lap on the sofa. He now had his own room and bed,

and I would often hop up there to sleep with him.

As Gip got sicker, he slept on a chair or the sofa. He seemed to have trouble sleeping. Each night I'd ask him if I could be with him, but he would shut the door on me, and I would go to Clement's room to sleep. On these nights, I missed my special person. On some mornings, though, he invited me into his room.

Then one day, Gip and Clement came back from a long doctor's appointment. They had been gone all morning and didn't get back until after lunch. I don't recall them ever being gone that long. Gip seemed unsettled. I heard him tell Clement that he felt like something bad had happened when he was on the gurney getting a full body scan. The technician pulled him off the gurney and then something just didn't feel right—it felt wrong.

Gip said he needed a hot bath. He stayed in the bathroom for an hour or so. When he finally came out, Gip looked so young and happy. He wore a yellow turtleneck and rust-colored pants and had a big smile on his face. Clement said he looked like he was seventeen again. At that point, I thought everything was going to be okay. Gip was going to be well and we could be happy again together.

The next night, Clement found his hospital test results online. The news was bad—Gip didn't have much time left on this earth. Clement had always hoped that he would get better. So many people were praying for him, and she simply did not want to think about her life without Gip.

Things went from bad to worse. Gip said he wasn't giving up and would keep on fighting, and Clement told him how much she needed him. She begged him not to leave her. I wanted to tell him that I needed him too and not to leave me. Gip was my person, and we needed to be with each other all my life. I tried to show it by staying by his side.

Then people started coming into the house. First, a young lady came and said she'd register them with some organization called "hospice." Trish, our neighbor, came over too. The three women talked for a long time, and the decision was made to put Gip on stronger medicine to help with his pain.

The following morning another lady, a nurse, showed up to help Gip. I could feel his pain and it scared me. The nurse gave him some medicine and then she left. The house felt kind of peaceful. Clement seemed lost and that scared me too.

They put a hospital bed in Gip's bedroom to make him more comfortable. I felt so sad because I couldn't help him. Gip had given me such a good life, had loved me, and had howled with me, and now I couldn't repay him and help him feel better.

Clement seemed like she was just going through the motions without knowing what to do or even what to expect next. I was worried for her. A neighbor told her to talk to Gip just like she normally would and to understand that death is like birth. It is a very natural thing and not to be feared. This eased Clement's mind.

Gip was in his new bed with a blanket wrapped around him. The medicine was strong but necessary. He looked peaceful and happy now.

I never thought much about where I came from, but this experience got me to thinking and believing there is a God. He created Gip, Clement, and me, and He put us all together. God must love all of us very much because He brought in people who provided medicine to take away Gip's pain.

God ushered Gip into His Heaven with dignity and peace. There was no long, drawn-out struggle for weeks, months, or years. There were three nights and part of a day, and then he was gone.

Clement let me come into his room and smell Gip's hand. I wanted to jump up and get in bed with him like I used to, but she held me back. Gip was gone. I knew he was gone.

My person was gone.

It took me a couple of days, but I realized Clement needed me now. My person was gone, but God gave me Clement to be my new person. I hadn't realized it before, but she had loved me all along. She seemed to have an overabundance of love for me now.

Clement cried when she discovered all the love notes Gip left for her in his office, but they were happy tears.

We're both struggling because Gip was so loved by both of us... and we are both a little lost. Clement seems lonely, but I am here for her.

Now we get up together in the morning, and she howls with me. I still go to doggy daycare, get treats when I come home, and then take a giant nap. It's not quite the same, but it's still good. I've grown to love Clement and want to be there for her.

We have more visitors since Gip went to Heaven. Some visitors I like and some I don't, but it is nice to meet new people.

I think we're going to make it. Clement sits around more often, and she cries sometimes. I am crying too, so I understand.

I bring her some of my toys to make her feel better, then we snuggle on the couch together. I offer her my soft tummy to scratch like I used to do for Gip when he was here.

I hope, with time, we will get a new life and enjoy things again. I think we will.

Love,

Luke XoXo

Author:
Luke Gibson

Luke decided to publish his book after a friend told him that his story would help others who are dealing with loss and grief. He is a first-time author.

Luke is a serious working dog, who puts guarding the house and yard first. When he is not working, he enjoys taking his person on a walk through the neighborhood, visiting with his best dog friends, Oliver the Basset Hound, Andrew the Lab/Golden Retriever mix, and Lu the Chihuahua. He loves riding in the back seat of the car with his head hanging out the window, ears flapping in the breeze, and sniffing all the captivating smells.

He can often be found napping on the leather sofa, dreaming about his next book.

~ Clement & Luke Gibson ~